JOURNAL FOR GIRLS

101 Thought Provoking Questions

Journal Questions for Girls

(Notebook)

By

Shalu Sharma

http://www.shalusharma.net
info@ShaluSharma.com
www.amazon.com/author/shalusharma

ISBN-13: 978-1517732905
ISBN-10: 1517732905

Other books by the author:

Self Discovery Journal: 121 Thought Provoking Questions: Journal Questions for Women (Notebook)

Gratitude Journal: Keep a Gratitude Journal and Turn Pain to Joy

This journal belongs to

Describe yourself in simple words or sentences.

What does your name mean?

Can you write how you are feeling today?

If you could change your name, what would it be?

When is your birthday and do you like celebrating it?

What are your best qualities?

Who do you like the most?

Who is your best friend?

If you were granted 3 wishes, what would you ask for?

Is there is one book you like to read again and again and why?

What do you think of your mum and dad?

What do you think of your sister or brother if you have any?

What annoys you the most and why?

What is your favourite color and why do you like it?

What is your favourite food and drink? What is good about it?

What is your most favourite thing about your school?

Who is your favourite teacher and why?

What are you really good at?

What do you like wearing the most and why?

What do you want to be when you grow up?

Which is your favourite toy and why?

What does it mean to be a good friend?

What do you think love means?

Tell me something that is really funny?

What makes you sad?

Which is your favourite animal and can you describe it?

What are you afraid off?

What do you like doing when you are not in school?

If you had one superpower what would that be?

What is the nicest thing a friend has done for you?

How would you describe your friends?

If I spent a day with you, how will you keep me from getting bored?

What is the most disgusting thing ever?

What is the hardest thing in the world for you to do?

If you could time travel where would you go?

What is the most amazing thing you have ever done?

If you could change one thing, what would that be?

When do you think a child becomes an adult?

Of all the things you are learning at school, what do you think will be the most useful?

What is the best gift you ever received on your birthday?

If you could become invisible for a day, what would you do?

Which is your favourite place in the whole world and why?

What types of books do you like reading?

How would you describe your country?

Which sports do you like to play?

Who do you look up to and why?

What are the things you can't live without?

Do you like singing in the shower?

Do you believe in God?

Do you like going on holidays?

What was your last dream about?

Write something about your favourite song.

What are the first things you do when you get up from bed?

What worries you the most?

Who do you love the most and why?

What makes you smile?

Are you scared of anything?

What are the best ways to help poor people of the world?

What are you most proud off?

What good habits you would have liked to have?

What do you think makes a good person?

What makes you laugh?

If you had a magic wand what would you change in an instant?

What are the things you like talking about?

What are the things important to you?

What have you been thinking about lately?

Is there anything that makes you angry?

What are the things you remember as a child?

What kinds of presents do you like getting?

Is there a place you would like to visit?

Do you remember all the planets of the solar system?

What makes earth the planet we live in so special?

Why do you think sugary things are bad for your teeth?

How are the guys treating you at school?

Who is your all time hero ever?

Which subject is your favourite at school?

If you had $50, what would you spend it on?

Why do you think it's bad to say swear words?

What is your favourite activity?

What activities do you enjoy doing with your family?

Do you pray to God and what do you ask for?

How would you describe a perfect day?

If you could keep a pet, what would you keep and how would you take care of it?

If you could change anything about your family, what would it be?

What is the proudest thing you have done in your life?

Do you have any jokes? Can you write one or two?

If you wrote a book, who would you have in it?

What is your favourite time of the year and why do you like it?

What is the silliest thing you have done?

Who is your best teacher at school and why?

Is there anything you wish you could tell your mother?

Do you ever feel like crying?

Do you know what the greenhouse effect is?

Can you name all the senses of the human body?

What makes mummy and daddy sad?

What is your best time of the day and why?

Do you think boys are different to girls and if so why?

What hair-style do you like and why?

What are your grandparents like?

Do you treat others nicely?

Have you expressed gratitude today?

50203106R00061

Made in the USA
San Bernardino, CA
15 June 2017